PLATO to DARWIN to DNA

A Brief History

Esther I. Muehlbauer

Kendall Hunt
publishing company

Cover image—Sarah Muehlbauer, photographer

Kendall Hunt
publishing company

www.kendallhunt.com
Send all inquiries to:
4050 Westmark Drive
Dubuque, IA 52004-1840

This book is dedicated to Eric—naturalist, horticulturalist, teacher, scholar, humanitarian—and my inspiration in the study and practice of life—And to our family, with love

TABLE OF CONTENTS

ABOUT THE AUTHOR

Esther Muehlbauer teaches biology and science writing at Queens College, of the City University of New York. She received her Ph.D. in biology from New York University, with a focus on salt marsh and estuarine ecology, and herpetology. She holds a BA from Queens College—where she studied biology and creative writing.

Introduction

Natural history is a story without an end, and with a somewhat nebulous beginning. Recounted by human narrators, the story's conception lies within the human mind itself—serving as both an instrument of interpretation and a product of life's evolutionary journey. Therefore, the telling of this primal story has changed throughout recorded time, throughout the varying developmental stages of human understanding. At any point in time, knowledge has been shaped by the tools available and the perceptions of their users. The earliest observers of the natural world had only their senses to work with, and were limited to visual, auditory, tactile, and olfactory descriptions perceived by the unaided human body. The development of the earliest microscope is an example of how a tool can alter fundamental human perceptions—the simple magnification of a living form reveals a previously unimagined complexity of structure.

The development of the "scientific process" too is an outgrowth of earlier, more primitive attempts to discern the true story. Fossil remains of human ancestors were first viewed as imperfect trials by a Creator, who later honed his craft to produce more successful modern humans. Ideas like this served as stepping stones to further exploration and interpretation, ultimately leading to modern geology and paleontology. Religion preceded science as an avenue for explaining the universe, its natural phenomena, and life forms. A very long period of transition followed, gradually and often painfully separating religious interpretation of the natural world, from scientific interpretation. Despite its hazy emergence, scientific observation can be traced back to ancient peoples, like the Paleolithic artists whose renderings of animals on cave walls captured the details of anatomical form. Similarly, the butchering of animals and ceremonial sacrifices led to knowledge of the internal structure of various organisms. Early agricultural practices like those in the Euphrates and Tigris valleys were based on an understanding of the seasons, and formulation of a timetable for planting and harvesting—an observation-based body of knowledge.

In the ancient world, biology unfurled incidentally, through the everyday inter-actions of people with their environment. Gradually and collectively a natural his-tory accrued. Individualism had not yet been born, and so artists, innovators, and philosophers were not singled out or celebrated among ancient peoples—ideas were sown and reaped communally. Therefore, we have no names for those who gave us the wheel, or the hunting bow, or who performed the first dissection, or first cataloged the ascent of spring. While accounts have been left that adequately describe the religious and ethical perceptions of the earliest cultures, the develop-ment of an individual philosophy, of which science is a part, had not yet come of age. An accurate written history often relies on earlier transcripts; however, in this most ancient period of human inquiry, there were no records that narrated scientific ideas or thought processes—and thus, insights are inferred. The earliest documents that show a continuous development of scientific ideas are found among the Greek culture, dating to about 500 BC, but even these accounts attribute much of their substance to more ancient civilizations such as those in Egypt and Mesopotamia.

A true scientific movement first arose in the second millennium, among the Ionians, a Greek-speaking tribe that colonized the shores of the Aegean Sea. This sea-faring people traded both goods and ideas with people from Egypt, Phoenicia, and India, and from this crossroads of communication, scientific thought was born. The Ionian merchant and politician, Thales (624–565 BC) is credited as the "father" of the systematic study of nature. By cataloging geometric and cyclic events in nature, Thales developed the idea of natural laws that maintain constancy in the living world amid an ever-changing backdrop. He described the cycling of water from the sky to the earth, from the earth to life forms, and back to the sky. From this beginning, a legacy of scientific study was generated.

The chapters to follow present a brief history in the development of natural science from this point onward, and a survey of some of the principle pioneers who shaped biological theory. However, the number of individuals who contributed to the evolution of scientific thought is immense—this attempt to catalog a few is at best fragmentary—but like the fossil record itself, it provides a framework for the realization of change.

CHAPTER 1
The Ancient Philosophers Set the Stage

Natural science was born from philosophy. The philosophers of the ancient world fathered many ideas on natural law, some of which dominated Western thought for the next 2000 years. In the 5th century BC, at the crossroads of Greek and Persian cultures, philosophy emerged as a serious academic discipline. Philosophical banter was no longer just a pastime of dabbling merchants or physicians—one could become a "professional thinker"—a respected philosopher. And many did. From Thales' calculations of the eclipses of the sun, and descriptions of water cycling through the biosphere, onward, a succession of Greek philosophers built upon the idea of "natural law," garnering concepts of the world through systematic observations. The goal of Thales and others of his generation was to find formulas to explain natural phenomena. They sought uniformity within a world of diversity. Thales was perhaps most successful at finding uniformity in his geometric studies, where he discovered rules regarding triangles—that the base angles of an isosceles triangle are equal, and that the sum of the angles of a triangle are equivalent to two right angles. Applying geometric principles to life situations, Thales was able to calculate the height of a pyramid by measuring its shadow, and the distance of a boat to the shore, by using the concept of similar triangles. This marked a beginning for the formulation of natural law based on observations of the world.

Heraclitus, a "professional thinker" of the period, promoted the controversial idea that everything in the world is continually changing, and that flux is the only universal reality. This idea of change is one that would remain controversial up through at least the 19th century. Heraclitus stated that "there's nothing is and nothing was, but everything's becoming." He viewed living organisms as a mixture of morphing essences like air and fire, and he interpreted birth and death as illusions in the spectrum of life where elements are continuously arranged and rearranged. Two-thousand years before Charles Darwin revolutionized biological science, by introducing the concept of change in his theory of evolution, Heraclitus proposed ideas on intrinsic change in living forms, and in all matter. These ideas were evaluated by subsequent generations of philosophers, such as Plato and his student, Aristotle, who became interested in this doctrine of flux.

THERE IS NOTHING PERMANENT EXCEPT CHANGE.

HERACLITUS

© YuryZap/Shutterstock.com

Plato interpreted Heraclitus' ideas on change to mean "that everything passes away and nothing remains," and that life itself is like the flow of a river, where you can't step into the same river twice. Plato saw two basic claims in Heraclitus' concept of flux. The first claim is that all matter undergoes progressive change, and even stable objects, like rocks and trees, are continuously having their matter replaced, like the water in a river. The second claim is that stable objects contain opposite properties at the same time, and are therefore "drawn together and drawn apart," creating internal flux. Internal flux can be seen in a printed letter of the alphabet that is both straight and curved if it is written with some straight lines and some curved lines; seawater can be good and bad at the same time, in that it's nurturing to marine organisms, and deadly to freshwater organisms. The "internal flux concept" questioned the validity of categorizing things based on distinct properties such as good or bad, straight or curved.

While Plato gave serious consideration to Heraclitus' views on change and stability, **Parmenides,** another philosopher of the period, was staunchly opposed to these ideas. Parmenides believed that change is not real, but simply the result of human interpretation. He rejected the use of human sensory perceptions as evidence of physical reality, since they often encompassed notions of change. Parmenides' overall rejection of the concept of change was based on the logic that change involves something becoming what it previously was not, and yet people are unable to conceive of *what is not*. According to this reasoning, "*what is not*"is nothing, and since nothing does not exist, then the concept of change cannot exist either. Despite his skepticism, Parmenides promoted the study of the universe (cosmology) by exploring the apparent properties of things, while at the same time denying that these appearances corresponded to any type of reality. He preferred to rely on human reason, rather than human senses for a realistic interpretation of the world. The naturalist successors to Parmenides were fully convinced of this logic, and tried to embrace cosmology without referring to the *"what is not"* concept that he had challenged.

Democritus, a contemporary of Socrates (470–399 BC), also relied largely on reason rather than the senses when assessing conflicting observations. Given a scenario where the same water felt cold to one individual and warm to another, Democritus concluded that both perceptions could not be true, and therefore they both must be false. He extended this logic to other sensory properties of matter such as sound, color, and smell, and theorized that matter cannot have any of these properties. Democritus was in conflict with his own conclusions, which he stated in a playful conversation between human senses and human reasons: "Wretched mind, do you take your proofs from us and then overthrow us? Our overthrow is your downfall." The philosopher, Protagoras, offered an alternate interpretation for Democritus' quandary. Protagoras concluded that if the wind appeared cold to one individual and warm to another, then neither had to be wrong, but the wind could be both cold and warm. Protagoras rejected Democritus' idea of an objective "nature," insisting that there is no reality free of human interpretation. Democritus did find a unique reality in the atom, which he described in terms of non-sensory attributes such as weight, shape, size, and motion. Curiously, he also believed that the characteristics of atoms create certain sensory effects, such as sharp atoms producing a bitter taste.

© Georgios Kollidas/Shutterstock.com

Democritus' most fundamental view of the atom was that it had eternal stability, and was the basic substance of all matter. He proposed that everything in the world is composed of indivisible, solid atoms and the voids that lie between them in meted spaces. The differences perceived among types of matter in the world, Democritus believed, are based solely on the motion and arrangement of atoms, not on qualitative differences. In this view, infinite cycles occur through time where atoms move and rearrange, and history endlessly repeats itself. Human beings and other living organisms are seen as temporary aggregations of atoms, and life and death are simply rearrangements of the same atoms. While this concept superficially mirrors Heraclitus' idea of a life–death continuum, Democritus' version does not include an innovation of form, but rather, an infinite replay of past forms. The strong parallels between Democritus' concepts of the atom and modern atomic theory are notable too, although Democritus' immediate ideological followers did little to promote these scientific ideas.

The importance of numbers in the study of nature, originated with the Pythagoreans (a school of thought named for its founder, Pythagoras, an Ionian, born in 580 B.C.). To the Pythagoreans, numbers had a real existence outside the human mind, which could be used to describe relationships between objects in the world. The poetic concept of the music of the spheres is based on a Pythagorean idea that the pitch of musical notes derives from a numerical ratio corresponding to the distance of heavenly bodies from the center of the world. Pythagorean mathematics was primarily geometry, and various theorems were formulated regarding triangles and other figures, including the well-known "Pythagorean Theorem" (that the square of the hypotenuse of a right triangle equals the sum of the squares of the other two sides). In addition, it was the Pythagoreans who first introduced the idea that the earth and planets are spheres, and who abandoned the view that the earth is the central point of the universe. Instead they considered the position of the earth to be similar to that of the other planets, and to revolve with them around a central fire—an idea that the renowned Polish astronomer, Nicholas Copernicus (1473–1543), built upon many centuries later.

CHAPTER 2
Ancient Cultures—Diverse Ideas

Although the roots of modern biology are most often traced to the philosophers of ancient Greece, there were other early cultures that developed significant ideas about humanity and its relationship to nature. The paucity of research on scientific ideas from diverse ancient cultures, such as those in China and India, stems in part from the oral tradition having maintained much of this knowledge, with less reliance on written accounts. But historically, Western scholarship has focused on ancient Greek culture—only more recently addressing the scientific traditions of other regions.

Chinese Culture

Early written documents from China were derived from alchemists, physicians, and philosophers. The *Taoist* alchemists were concerned with finding elixirs that could grant health, longevity, and immortality, and were dispensed by practicing herbalists and folk-healers. Zhuangzi, a Taoist philosopher of the 4th century BC, had theorized astute ideas about evolutionary processes, stating that species were not fixed entities but developed variable characteristics in response to changing environments.

Zhuangzi's philosophy grew out of the Spring and Autumn Periods in Chinese History (771–476 BC), and the ideas of Laozi, an earlier philosopher of this period. *Dao (the Way)* was the central idea in Laozi's philosophy, and was considered to be the root of the earth, the heavens, and everything in between. *The Way* followed nature, revealing its truth, and ascribing a natural character to all creatures, including humanity and its societies. It was a conservation-oriented philosophy, contending that people follow the ways of Nature, without placing too many demands upon it. Zhuangzi expanded on the interpretation of *The Way*, regarding everything in nature as a transient phenomenon. A prolific writer, he authored numerous philosophical texts, including one with a chapter on "Butterflies and Dreams," where the idea of natural transformation is depicted. The following passage from this work describes the concept of "Tao"—that all Nature and Heaven, humans, and living creatures exist in a continuous state of transformation.

> Once Zhuangzi dreamt he was a butterfly, a butterfly flitting and fluttering around, happy with himself and doing as he pleased. He didn't know he was Zhuangzi. Suddenly he woke up and there he was, solid and unmistakable Zhuangzi. But he didn't know if he was Zhuangzi who had dreamt he was a butterfly, or a butterfly dreaming he was Zhuangzi. Between Zhuangzi and a butterfly, there must be *some* distinction! This is called the Transformation of Things. (tr. Burton Watson, 1968)

© Charlesimage/Shutterstock.com

Within classical Chinese philosophy, the concept of *Yin and Yang* and its *five phases* (*Earth, Metal, Fire, Wood, and Water*) emerged from ancient scientific and medical practices as a prominent ideology. *Yin and Yang* explained the unity of life, nature, health, and disease. *The five phases*, sometimes regarded as analogous to the four elements in ancient Greek science (Earth, Air, Fire, and Water), indicate transition and change, in contrast to the stability of elements in Greek thought. In a pattern of change, the *Five Phases* interact with one another in a continuous cycle:

Water quells *Fire;*
Fire melts *Metal;*
Metal cuts *Wood;*
A *Wood* plow turns *Earth;*
Earth halts *Water.*

Chinese scholars have ascribed the principle of Yin and Yang to everything in creation—the origin of life, and the cause of all transformation. While it is difficult to translate the precise meaning of Yin and Yang from the original Chinese, the terms are interpreted as the dualism of the universe in pairs of opposites. Yin, the feminine aspect, represents water, the earth, the moon, and the night—it is characterized by all that is light, slow, soft, yielding, diffuse, cold, wet, and passive. Yang, the masculine aspect, represents fire, the sky, the sun, and the day—it embraces all that is dark, fast, hard, solid, focused, hot, dry, and aggressive. Medical knowledge based on Yin and Yang philosophy was developed in ancient China to describe the physiological functions of the human body. While Western physiology was not born until the 17th century, with the work of William Harvey (1578–1657), ancient Chinese scholars, thousands of years earlier, realized physiological relationships, such as those of the human circulatory system—involving the heart, the pulse, and the circulation of blood.

Ancient Indian Traditions

Evidence for mathematical and scientific knowledge of the Indus Valley Civilization has come from archaeological excavations at the Harappa and Mohenjo Daro sites, where planned cities flourished in the Indian subcontinent over 4500 years ago. Mathematics and geometry were highly developed fields that were applied to practical applications in building design. For example, bricks were manufactured with dimensions in a 4:2:1 ratio, to provide stability in built structures. Astronomical musings, while intertwined with the religious literature, revealed concepts about the origin of the universe, the spherical nature of the earth, and a calendar year divided into 12 equal parts.

© suronin/Shutterstock.com

Inspired religious writing from the Indus Valley civilization documents considerable knowledge about the nature of the universe and the human condition. In Hindu religion, the god Brahma, referred to as "The First Teacher of the Universe," was credited with composing the great epic, *Ayurveda—The Science of Life*. Passed down through the oral tradition by generations of sages, this work was ultimately recorded in written texts, and provides insights into ancient Indian medical practices, physiology, psychology, embryology, and alchemy.

One of the oldest traditions of organized medicine is evidenced in the Ayurveda, which describes the human body as being composed of three humors (wind, blood, and phlegm), five elements (earth, water, fire, wind, and empty space), and seven basic tissues. Bodily functions were additionally supported by five specific *winds*, a *vital soul,* and an *inmost soul.* The humors referenced in the Ayurveda exist in a harmonious balance to support life and strongly parallel the humors described in ancient Greek medicine, but offer a more detailed perspective.

The life processes of reproduction and embryological development were given substantial thought within the writings of the Ayurveda. Living things were in fact classified based on their means of reproduction and birth. The four categories of classification were:

1. life forms born from the womb
2. life forms that hatch from eggs
3. life forms that arise from heat and moisture
4. life forms that develop from seeds

The Ayurveda stated that conception occurred within the womb by materials from the male and female parents, with the addition of an "external self" or *spirit.* Descriptions of the stages of pregnancy and the development of a child from an amorphous jelly-like mass were also detailed in these writings.

A sophisticated surgical tradition arose in the Indus Valley Civilization even though religious doctrine forbade the use of the knife on human cadavers. Despite this limitation, descriptive maps of the human body were accurately created, and included a system for locating "vital points." These points identified regions of the body that if injured, could result in extensive bleeding, chronic pain, or even death. Ancient physicians and surgeons were guided by the knowledge of vital points when performing surgeries, treating wounds, or blood-letting. In fact, some contemporary healers still refer to maps of "vital points" of the human body for treatments such as massage therapy.

Mesopotamia

The cyclic flooding of the river valleys in Mesopotamia and Egypt dictated the pattern of life in these regions. All aspects of existence, from agriculture to engineering, were carefully timed to the river cycle, under the direction of knowledgeable priests and nobles. This ultimately determined the way people thought about nature. Knowledge of biological and cosmological events served a pragmatic purpose rather than an abstract subject for academic inquiry. Similarly, the myths of these civilizations revolved around the separation of dry land from water, and the derivation of living creatures from the mud. Through the mythology, people could understand the problems of irrigation and flood control, and the necessity of storing food during harsh periods.

© sondem/Shutterstock.com

About 3500 years ago, the Mesopotamian peoples from Sumer (now Iraq) began recording the movement of celestial bodies with great mathematical accuracy. Astronomical records left on thousands of clay tablets, detailed the precise movements of the moon, the stars, and the planets. Contemporary Western calendars are still based on the ancient Mesopotamian astronomical calculations of the seven-day week, the lunar month, and the solar year. From these data, astronomers of the time, like Kidinnu (an astronomer/mathematician, and one of the few recorded names), were able to calculate the length of daylight through the changing seasons, and to predict events such as the appearance and disappearance of the moon, and the recurring eclipses of the sun and the moon. While these realizations provided the basis for a scientific world view, in subsequent generations, the Mesopotamian civilization became more astrology based, moving away from rational science, and toward a greater interest in astrological omens and horoscopes.

© kactana/Shutterstock.com

Ancient Egypt

In a stanza from Homer's epic poem, the *Odyssey* (800 BC), it is written:

In Egypt, the men are more skilled in medicine than any of human kind –
The Egyptians were skilled in medicine more than any other art –

Knowledge of ancient Egyptian science and medicine began to be revealed in the 19th century, with the translation of the Rosetta stone hieroglyphics in 1882, and the subsequent translation of Egyptian medical papyri. Interest in "Egyptology" during this period led to the discovery of many ancient medical documents, including the "Edwin Smith Papyrus," which is considered to be the first medical textbook on surgery. This work details anatomical observations and information on the diagnosis, treatment, and prognosis of various ailments, and is perhaps the earliest document that attempts to describe the human brain. Imhotep (2650–2600 BC) of the 3rd-century dynasty in Egypt is credited as the original author of the

Edwin Smith Papyrus, as well as the founder of ancient Egyptian medicine. He is also sometimes granted the title of "first" architect, engineer, and physician in early history. (The original Edwin Smith Papyrus is now on view at the Brooklyn Children's Museum in New York City.)

Based on the ancient Egyptian's close association with the Nile River, the physicians of the time likened the body's systems of "channels" to the flow of the river. The analogy was furthered in terms of medical treatments—for example, laxatives were administered if bodily "channels" were blocked, just as agricultural crops needed restoration when the flow of the Nile was stopped. Significant knowledge into the overall morphology of the body and the function of organs was gained through surgery and the practice of autopsy and mummification in religious ritual. Most organ functions were correctly identified, although there appeared to be some confusion between the heart and the brain—with their presumed functions being switched.

© stesharp/Shutterstock.com

CHAPTER 3
Socrates, Plato, and Aristotle—A Lasting Legacy

The ideas of Socrates (470–399 BC), Plato (429–347 BC), and Aristotle (384–322 BC), on natural philosophy, were the most enduring influences on Western "biological" thought to emerge from ancient Greece, and the classical world. Building on the work of the Pre-Socratic philosophers, who described the world primarily in material terms ("materialism"), this new generation of philosophers, beginning with Socrates, envisioned a world with both physical and spiritual elements. Man was viewed as a composite of entwined components—a dualism of body and soul.

Socrates

While Socrates is often considered a "moral philosopher," rather than a "natural philosopher," his ideas impacted on two realms of thought—philosophy and natural science. Socrates left no written accounts, but his ideology survived in the work

© Ververidis Vasilis/Shutterstock.com

of his student, Plato. In the form of "Socratic dialogues," Plato drafted exchanges between his mentor, Socrates, and members of Athenian society. The questioning technique in these dialogues reveals Socrates' pedagogy—that knowledge should be elicited from the student, rather than provided by the teacher. Socrates believed that knowledge embodied the good in the world, whereas ignorance embodied evil, and that it was his personal role in life to lead others toward knowledge through a process of introspection.

In a discussion of different forms of knowledge ("arts"), the following passage from Plato's dialogue *Ion,* illustrates the "Socratic method" of instruction. Here Socrates questions Ion, a performer, about who is more knowledgeable about being a chariot driver—a performer, reciting an epic poem about a charioteer, or an actual charioteer?

Socrates. If the subject of knowledge were the same, there would be no meaning in saying that the arts were different - if they gave the same knowledge. For example, I know that here are five fingers, and you know the same. And if I were to ask whether you and I became acquainted with this fact by the help of the same art of arithmetic, you would acknowledge that we did?

Ion. Yes.

Socrates. Tell me, then, what I was intending to ask you—whether this holds universally? Must the same art have the same subject of knowledge, and different arts other subjects of knowledge?

Ion. That is my opinion, Socrates.

Socrates. Then he who has no knowledge of a particular art will have no right in judgment of the sayings and doings of that art?

Ion. Very true.

Socrates. Then which will be a better judge of the lines which you were reciting from Homer, you or the charioteer*?

Ion. The charioteer.

Socrates. Why, yes, because you are a rhapsode** and not a charioteer.

Ion. Yes.

Socrates. And the art of the rhapsode is different from that of the charioteer?

Ion. Yes.

Socrates. And if a different knowledge, then a knowledge of different matters?

Ion. True.

(*Charioteer: the driver of a chariot)
(**Rhaposde: a person who recited epic poems from memory as a profession, in ancient Greece.)

In terms of its application to scientific reasoning, the Socratic technique of eliciting knowledge through questioning was later realized to be an antecedent of the "scientific method," where alternate hypotheses are evaluated and tested. The Socratic method allows for refinement of hypotheses by steadily eliminating ideas that are contradictory or lack validity. Through this process of elimination, the wisdom of the famous *Socratic paradox*—"I know that I know nothing," could have arisen.

Plato

© Anastasios71/Shutterstock.com

Plato, like his mentor Socrates, developed concepts in the realm of "moral philosophy," relating to theology, politics, and ethics—concepts that also impacted on the development of Western scientific reasoning and study. He strived to develop a comprehensive theory that uncovered discrepancies in human thought. In his *Doctrine of Ideas*, Plato attempted to differentiate between things that exist independently from human sensory perception—and those that rely on the senses for description. Building on the philosopher Heracleitus' idea of flux—that the perceptions of the senses are changing, and therefore unreliable—Plato's *Ideas* represented those entities that can "stand alone" and are defined. According to this doctrine, ideas of the mind are more concrete than impressions of the physical world that are sensory-based.

Gathering thoughts from many philosophers and mathematicians of his day, such as Hippocrates and the Pythagoreans, Plato founded the Academy, situated among a grove of olive trees in Athens. Here he lectured on philosophy, with the ultimate goal of imparting his ideas to society by teaching a new generation of political philosophers. Plato's search for truth was based on a belief that knowledge could be gained through reason rather than observations of nature. He interpreted the relationships among living organisms as a reverse evolutionary process, where other species of animals were derived from man through a gradual degradation of form. Viewing life, from a teleological perspective (e.g., having purpose), Plato believed that the study of nature would ultimately reveal an intelligent design to the universe. Each living species was viewed as a unique form, and the individuals of the species were mere representations of the idealized form. This notion grew into the concept of *essentialism,* where each species was considered to have a particular *essence,* and variations among individuals of the species were viewed as unimportant imperfections. Essentialism had a dramatic impact on natural science for the next 2000 years—up until Darwin's theory of evolution revolutionized thought in the 19th century. Until then the world view was dominated by religious doctrine (validated by essentialism), that species were independently placed on the Earth by a Creator, and remained unchanged henceforth.

Aristotle

© thelefty/Shutterstock.com

Plato's celebrated student and disciple, Aristotle, contributed significantly to the historical development of biology—reinterpreting, and building on Plato's concept of essentialism, and his "theory of forms," and founding his own school in Athens—the Lyceum. Aristotle's important writings in natural history include four books, usually referred to by their Latin names—*De anima* ("On the Soul"), *Historia animalium* ("Natural History of Animals"), *De generationae animalium* ("On the Generation of Animals"), and *De partibus animalium* ("On the Parts of Animals"). In his book "On the Soul," Aristotle broaches the eternal questions—What is life? When does life begin? He defines life as having "the power of self-nourishment and of independent growth and decay." As for the point at which life begins, Aristotle describes the egg or "germ" as not living until after fertilization, when it becomes capable of developing a soul. In a frequently quoted passage from *De anima,* Aristotle writes:

> The term life is used in various senses. If life be present in but a single one of these senses, we speak of a thing as alive. Thus, there is intellect, sensation, motion from place to place and rest, the activity concerned with nutrition, and the processes of decay and growth. Plants have life, for they have within themselves a faculty whereby they grow and decay. They grow and live so long as they are capable of absorbing nourishment. In virtue of this principle, all living things live, whether animals or plants, but it is sensation which primarily constitutes the animal and justifies us in speaking of an "*animal soul*". For, provided they have sensation, creatures, even if incapable of movement, are called animals. As the nutritive faculty may exist, as in plants, without touch or any form of sensation, so also touch may exist apart from other senses.

Aristotle's classification of life forms relates to the type of soul an organism possesses. He diverges from Plato's concept that body and soul are distinct entities, and rather describes the soul as "that which gives the form or actuality in living things." According to Aristotle, the soul does not have a separate existence. He catalogs the soul as one of three types—"vegetative," "animal," and "rational"—arranged in an order of increasing consciousness, with the "rational" or intellectual soul, being unique to man. This ascending scale is part of what has come to be known as Aristotle's *Scala naturae*—"Ladder of Nature."

Aristotle was an astute observer of nature. This is evident in his writings, such as *The Natural History of Animals,* compiled from Aristotle's original observations and dissections, along with insights from farmers, fishermen, and hunters. He believed that every organism had "something natural and something beautiful" to reveal. While Aristotle realized the necessity of a system of classification for life forms, he did not attempt to serve as a true taxonomist, but rather as a philosopher, suggesting possible systems for grouping organisms. Echoing Plato's concept of "essentialism," Aristotle viewed species as bearing an eternal essence, with individual variations, mere accidental imperfections. He delineated only two categories of classification—*genos* and *eidos*—roughly equivalent to genus and species.

While Aristotle's Ladder of Nature superficially appears like an evolutionary progression, it does not support the view that life forms are related by descent. However, it does indicate a realization that organisms exhibit degrees of complexity that can be sequenced by varying gradations. Exploring this idea in *The History of Animals*, Aristotle writes:

> Nature proceeds by little and little from things lifeless to animal life, so that it is impossible to determine the exact line of demarcation, nor on which side an intermediate form should lie. Thus, next after lifeless

things in the upward scale, comes the plant. Of plants one will differ from another as to its amount of apparent vitality. In a word, the whole plant kind, while devoid of life as compared with the animal, is yet endowed with life as compared with other corporeal entities. Indeed there is observed in plants a continuous scale of ascent toward the animal.

Aristotle gave considerable thought to the concept of change—one of the cornerstones of modern biology. He described four causes for change as—formal, final, material, and efficient. Using the example of a seed developing into a plant, the "formal" cause would be the internal drive of the seed to mature. The "final" cause for change is the seed's tendency to reach its fully developed state, and the "material" cause describes the substance of change—the actual plant tissue that grows and derives from the seed. Lastly, Aristotle's "efficient" cause is a prior event leading up to the change—such as the seed being planted and then germinating.

Aristotle's writings exhibit a depth and breadth of biological thought unmatched by his predecessors' work. Some of his most notable studies include:

- Records of the breeding habits of 540 species of animals.
- Embryological studies of developing chicks.
- A study of the habits of squid and octopuses.
- Identifying the mammalian nature of porpoises and dolphins.

Aristotle also introduced the technique of using diagrams to illustrate anatomical and physiological systems. In exploring concepts such as heredity, generation, and sex, he provided the earliest presentation of ideas central to modern biology. While Aristotle's approach to biological study was largely observation-based, many subsequent generations of scholars fixated on his writings in lieu of making their own observations. This overreliance on Aristotle's accounts, rather than his methodology, significantly stagnated development in the biological sciences.

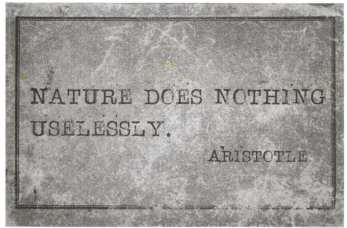

NATURE DOES NOTHING USELESSLY.
ARISTOTLE

© YuryZap/Shutterstock.com

CHAPTER 4
Roman Influences—
A Practical Approach

© Konstantin Aksenov/Shutterstock.com

During the 2nd century BC, the Greek cities that had been prominent cultural centers came under Roman rule. Although Greek knowledge in science and other academic disciplines was assimilated into Roman culture during the period from the 2nd century BC to the 2nd century AD, the Roman world advanced only modestly in biological and medical knowledge—fostering greater expertise in practical applications such as sanitation and agriculture. Agriculture in ancient Rome became a way of life. Cicero, the famous Roman philosopher and politician, in his treatise *On Duties,* stated that "of all the occupations by which gain is secured, none is better than agriculture, none more profitable, none more delightful, none more becoming of a free man." The Roman utilitarian view of nature grew, in part, from *Stoicism,* a prevalent philosophy among the governing classes that stressed the value of logic—to follow where reason leads.

Columella and Cato

Lucius Junius Moderatus Columella, a 2nd-century AD biologist, developed a significant body of work on agriculture, writing a 12-volume farming handbook, *De Re Rustica* ("On Agriculture"), one of the most in-depth studies of Roman agriculture. The volumes address not only farming practices for main-stay crops such as spelt, but detailed advice on *viticulture* (grape-growing) and wine-making. Columella provides information on which soil types produce the best wine grapes and devotes an entire volume to the technical aspects of winemaking. His instructions on the practice of boiling grapes in a lead vessel to enhance sweetness may have had the unfortunate consequence of causing cases of lead-poisoning. However, other *best practices* of Columella's viticulture are still evident in modern vineyards, from vine-staking and trellising techniques to pruning and grape-selection. Contemporary *Cabernet* grapes are believed to be derived from the ancient Roman *Balisca* and *Biturica* varieties described by Columella.

Portrait of Lucius Junius Moderatus Columella from Jean de Tournes, *Insignium aliquot virorum icones*, **Lyon, 1559**

Significant writings on Roman agriculture are also credited to Marcus Porcius Cato (234–149 BC), a Roman statesman, often referred to as *Cato the Sensor* or *Cato the Elder*. His treatise, *De Agri Cultura* ("On Farming"), describes the worth of agricultural plantings from the most highly ranked vineyards, to olive orchards, grain fields, and lastly acorn woodlands. Cato's agricultural handbook also provides a set of guidelines on animal husbandry, and insights into "country life" in the 2nd century BC, including recipes for pickles and baked goods. This text is the oldest surviving prose work written in Latin, and served as a utilitarian guide for Romans at a time when agriculture was a rapidly developing practice.

Cato's "medical" writings contained less enduring ideas—assemblages of magic formulas of the type that had been dismissed by Hippocrates generations earlier when he replaced superstition with rational observation-based methods. However, there were other medical documents from the Roman period that were more observation-based, such as *De Medicina* ("On Medicine"), one of the earliest medical encyclopedias. Compiled by Aulus Census, a contemporary of Christ, *De Medicina* detailed the structure of human anatomical parts including the eye, ear, and teeth. *De Virtutibus Aquae Vitae* ("The Virtues of Alcohol"), written by Alderotti Thaddeus in the 1st century AD, was an observation-based compendium describing medical uses for alcohol, such as its utility in reducing fevers.

Marcus Porcius Cato

Lucretius

The Roman philosopher Titus Lucretius Carus (99–44 BC) authored the poetic *De Rerum Natura* ("On the Nature of Things")—a monumental literary work that has impacted on a scientific world view. *De Rerum Natura* is essentially a six-volume epic poem that explores the principles of atomism (that nature is composed of atoms and voids), the nature of the mind and soul, thought and sensation, and concepts on the development of the world and worldly phenomena. Lucretius presented an *Epicurean* view to his readers by forwarding empirical evidence rather than divine intervention and describing a universe that functions according to physical principles.

Evolutionary ideas have also been interpreted in Lucretius' writings. He describes "a ladder of nature," similar to Aristotle's *Scala naturae*, beginning with plants and ascending to animals of increasing complexity:

> Even as down and hair and bristles are first formed on the limbs of beasts . . . so the newborn earth raised up herbage and shrubs first, and thereafter the races of mortal things.

It remains unclear whether Lucretius was describing evolutionary descent in a true Darwinian sense; however, it is apparent that he believed in a concept of change in life forms and in the earth itself, which he stated was destined to change and ultimately perish. Lucretius' writings clearly promote the concept of *spontaneous generation*—that life can arise from non-life given appropriate conditions—an idea that was propagated by many biologists up until the mid-19th century when it was finally disproven by Louis Pasteur. In *De Rerum Natura*, Lucretius described spontaneous generation in the statement:

> Even now many animals spring forth from the earth, formed by rains and the heat of the sun.

Lucretius used the philosophy of atomism to explain everything from the history of the universe to the structure of human society—stating that all are composed of atoms, and all are products of nature, including human beings, their souls, and dreams.

Lucretius was critical of Roman civilization, advocating for simplicity in life over advancing technologies, and admonished mixing religious doctrine with mainstream aspects of society. In turn, Christian theologians were skeptical of the Epicurean philosophy that Lucretius promoted and few copies of *De Rerum Natura* lasted into the Middle Ages. However, during the Renaissance, Lucretius' work was rediscovered, and used as a model of exemplary scientific writing. The presentation of ideas was so compelling that *De Rerum Natura* inspired generations of thinkers including philosophers like Bruno and Dante, and the scientist, Dalton, who many centuries later developed his atomic theory by building on Lucretius' concept of atoms.

Pliny

Gaius Plinius Secundus (Pliny) (23–79 AD) was a notable Roman biologist, who like Lucretius strived to rid society of superstition by offering explanations of worldly phenomena through the study of nature. Pliny was an "encyclopedist" whose culminating 37-volume *Historia Naturalis* ("Natural History") encapsulated the writings of a few hundred Greek and Roman authors from over 2000 works. It remained a staple biological and agricultural reference through the Byzantine era and into the 16th century. Pliny's "Natural History" includes information on diverse topics, ranging from medicine and economics to comparative anatomy, physiology, and zoology, with detail given to the behavior and anatomy of farm animals.

Although many of Pliny's anatomical descriptions seem to be reworked versions of Aristotle's, he did include some original observations on numerous plants and animals, (particularly bees)—even describing how organs vary in size and structure from one species of organism to another. The botanical themes of the work address agriculture, horticulture, and forestry, the medicinal uses of plants, and derived products such as wine.

Pliny insightfully categorizes humans together with animals, although he maintains that other animals have the primary purpose of serving man. This theme of nature existing for human use is one that recurs throughout Pliny's "Natural History"— "Nature and the Earth . . . fill us with admiration . . . as we contemplate the great variety of plants and find they are created for the wants or enjoyments of mankind."

© Morphart Creation/Shutterstock.com

Galen

Aelius Galenus (Galen) (129–200AD), a Greek-born physician, was one of the great influences on biological thinking and medical practice to emerge from the Roman era. His ideas on physiology and anatomy helped to define the disciplines, and despite some misconceptions on physiology, Galen's writings remained influential up through the 19th century.

Galen rejuvenated the field of anatomy, which had greatly declined in the Roman era, since dissections of the human body were no longer practiced. In lieu, Galen performed accurate physiological and anatomical studies on animals, such as pigs and goats, the Barbary Macaque and other apes, that he noted were structurally similar to humans. Based on these studies, Galen created detailed diagrams of the human circulatory, respiratory, and nervous systems. Through a series of experiments, Galen was able to conclude that the brain controls muscles via cranial and peripheral nerves, and he created an accurate map of the brain, detailing neural pathways that are in agreement with modern neurology. While his analysis of the circulatory system was less accurate—as in descriptions of both veins and arteries carrying blood away from the heart, Galen corrected flaws in earlier physiological interpretations, such as Aristotle's notion that the heart is the site where nerves originate. Galen was an early proponent of the scientific method, urging his readers to "test" the writings and ideas of even the great physicians and scientists of the day, by observing nature directly.

Galen served as an inspiration many generations later, in the 16th and 17th centuries, during the Scientific Revolution—when there was a renewed interest to reassess scientific concepts and to build.

© Everett Historical/Shutterstock.com

CHAPTER 5
When It Was Dark—Medieval Knowledge

© littleny/Shutterstock.com

   The "Dark Ages," a period historically referenced by stagnation in academic inquiry following the fall of Rome in 476 AD, was in many ways illuminated. While European Medieval society (500–1500 AD) did not foster original research in biology and medicine, significant advances were made in technology, construction, and agriculture. Windmill and watermill designs were perfected, textile production was enhanced, and new crop varieties were introduced. By the 12th century, these changes had dramatically impacted on society—leading to increased food production, population growth, and the formation of urban centers. A renewed interest in the translation of ancient Greek texts was also transforming European culture, making subjects like astronomy, mathematics, and medicine current.

The University

Perhaps the most significant academic development of the period was the formation of the medieval university, a construct that differed from earlier more informal communities of scholars. The university was centered around formal lectures and a standardized curriculum, often attracting students from other countries who wanted to study with a prominent scholar in a particular field. Although the literate and educated made up a very small percentage of the population, by the 13th century, there were 20 European universities scattered within France, Italy, Spain, and England and 80 by the close of the Middle Ages.

Religious authority still bore its imprint on academic study. Thomas Aquinas' edited writings of Aristotle were popular among both scholars and theologians—promoting a "geocentric" world view (that the earth lies at the center of the universe), and a hierarchy of life forms, as presented in Aristotle's *Scala Naturae* (The Great Chain of Being)—a linear progression from inanimate minerals, to fossils (considered intermediate between the nonliving and living), to plants, animals, humans, celestial beings, and ultimately God. While "The Great Chain of Being" defined a static progression of forms, it did provide a theoretical framework for later evolutionary ideas to be incorporated into a developmental sequence from the simple to the more complex. The 13th-century scholar Albertus Magnus wrote that:

Nature does not make kinds separate without making something intermediate between them; for nature does not pass from extreme to extreme without an intermediate.

(Translated in Lovejoy, 136: 79)

Nicolas of Cusa, a 15th-century scholar, expressed a similar sentiment in his work, *De Docta Ignorentia* (1440):

All things different are linked together. There is in the genera of things such a connection between the higher and the lower that they meet in a common point; such an order obtains among species that the highest species of one genus coincides with the lowest of the next higher genus, in order that the universe may be one, perfect, continuous.

(Translated in Lovejoy, 1936: 80)

"Scholasticism" framed the educational structure of the medieval university—a philosophy that ancient works constituted the entirety of knowledge, with little room for fresh observations and ideas. The 13th-century scholars, like Albertus Magnus, wrote interpretations of Aristotle's work that remained largely in line with Church teachings. Breaking from the mold to some degree, Magnus described several new plant species, in addition to his full commentary on Aristotle's seminal writings on plants, animals, and minerals (in *De Vegetabilas et Plantis, De Animalibus, and De Mineralibus*).

Roger Bacon and Hildegard

© ArtMari/Shutterstock.com

Medieval scholar, Roger Bacon (1214–1292) has been referred to as the "first modern scientist," based on his use of empirical methods to study nature, and as an early proponent of the "Scientific Method"—gaining knowledge through experimentation. Bacon called for reforms in theological study, urging theologians to study science by observation and experimentation, rather than a blind acceptance of earlier ideas. One of Bacon's most celebrated studies was on optics—which he included in his text, *Opus Majus*—providing a discussion of the anatomy of the eye and brain, the physiology of eyesight, the processes of reflection and diffraction, and the mechanics of mirrors, lenses, and magnifying glasses. Other scientific contributions credited to Roger Bacon are the formula for gunpowder and a manual on alchemy, *Speculum Alchemiae* ("The Mirror of Alchemy")—a treatise on the origins and composition of metals. Roger Bacon remains a "folk hero" in contemporary culture, a character in Thomas Costain's popular book, *The Black Rose* (1945), and in the video game "Shadow Hearts" (2001), where Bacon is a 700-year-old immortal scientist/alchemist.

© daseugen/Shutterstock.com

Hildegard of Bingen (1098–1179) was a German medieval scholar—one of the few women from the era who entered academia despite significant gender barriers. Her scholarship embraced diverse fields, from botanical and medicinal texts to liturgical songs, poems, and theological writings. Known in her day as a mystic and visionary, and recognized by the Roman Catholic Church as a saint, Hildegard has gained considerable appreciation by recent historians of science and medicine. (Her "visionary" abilities have been attributed to classic migraine symptoms by modern medical evaluators.) Much of her medical expertise was derived from working in the herbal garden and infirmary at a monastery. Hildegard's *Liber Simplicis Medicinae* (The Book of Simple Medicine), also known as *Physica*, is a nine-volume work that describes herbal and medicinal properties of plants, animals, and minerals. Her second work, *Liber Compositae Medicinae* (The Book of Compound Medicine, also known as *Causae et Curae*), discusses the link between the human body and the natural world, focusing on the causes and cures for various diseases, and home remedies for injuries such as burns, cuts, and fractures. Hildegard's approach to medicine was like that of a gardener, building on the relationship between organism and environment. Considered to be the first German texts on natural history, Hildegard's writings also provide some of the earliest listings of local plant names.

Islamic Science

From the 8th through the 13th-centuries, scientific scholarship flourished in the Islamic world—during a period known as the Golden Age of Islam. Beginning with the reign of the caliph, Harun ar-Rashid, scholars from around the world flocked to "The House of Wisdom" in Baghdad, to gather and translate ancient manuscripts into Arabic. Arab scientists were particularly interested in optics, chemistry, alchemy, medicine, and pharmacology, and utilized the experimental approach in the preparation and testing of drugs. As a precursor to Darwin's 19th-century concept of "natural selection," introduced in *The Origin of Species* (1859)—A 9th-century scholar, al-Jahiz, wrote of "a struggle for existence" in his text, *Kitab al-Hayawan* (Book of Animals).

Building on the works of the ancient scholars Hippocrates and Galen, Arab medical pioneers expanded the repertoire of knowledge. A few notable medical scientists were Yuhanna ibn Massuwayh, who developed dissection techniques and described allergies; Rhazes, who identified differences between smallpox and measles, introduced the use of mercurial ointments and compresses in surgery, and wrote a notable 30-volume medical encyclopedia, *Al-Hawi*; Az-Zarawi, the "father of modern surgery" is also credited with identifying sex-linked inheritance in hemophilia; and Avicenna, who described anthrax and tuberculosis and advocated for a holistic approach to treating patients—he also authored *al-Qanun fil Tibb* ("The Canon of Medicine"), which served as the authoritative text on medicine for the next 500 years.

Technology also flourished during the Golden Age of Islam, giving rise to new techniques for irrigation, such as underground channels, and the development of windmills and waterwheels—which had a lasting impact on future generations.

© Everett Historical/Shutterstock.com

Suggested Readings

Zirkle, Conway "Natural Selection before *The Origin of Species*." *Proceedings of the American Philosophical Society* 84(1) (1941): 71–123.

© arousa/Shutterstock.com

CHAPTER 6
The Renaissance and Biology

© QQ7/Shutterstock.com

The European Renaissance—a cultural and intellectual "rebirth" during the 14th to 17th centuries—elicited new interpretations of the natural world. It was a period of transformation from an ancient to a modern world, prompting altered perspectives in art, architecture, literature, and science. The backdrop for this rebirth rested in part on changes in social stratification and an emerging sense of individualism—spurring greater creativity and experimentation. Oscar Wilde, the 19th-century writer/poet stated that "art is individualism," and that its value lies in seeking to "disturb monotony" and halt "the reduction of man to the level of a machine." Thus, in the Renaissance, a sense of nonconformity developed as a motivator for experimentation in art and science.

Cultural enhancement evolved together with inventions like the printing press and the discovery of new sea routes—enabling an exploration of the New World and other "remote" regions. These Renaissance explorations confronted natural philosophers and physicians with a plethora of uncataloged plants and animals, as well as previously unknown diseases.

Francis Bacon

© Everett Historical/Shutterstock.com

The scientific philosopher Francis Bacon (1561–1626) cited the combined effects of gunpowder, printing, and the compass as the most significant developments of the Renaissance. Bacon believed that these three inventions ultimately "changed the appearance and state of the whole world." The manufacture of gunpowder during the Renaissance gave military power to those who controlled its production, and therefore the rise of the modern state is directly linked to firearm development. While both gunpowder manufacture and printing (and paper-making) originated in China, their appearance in Europe accelerated the changes taking place during the Renaissance. A landmark printing event—Johann Gutenburg's letter, printed with movable type in 1454—heralded a new age in European communications. Printing presses became mainstays throughout Europe by 1500, creating a vernacular litera-ture and an efficient mechanism for the transmission of ideas throughout society. As for the magnetic compass—refinement of this 12th-century invention during the Renaissance allowed for more precise navigation by sea and the subsequent discov-ery of new regions and resources.

Francis Bacon himself was a significant force in the development of Renaissance ideas—establishing the framework for the "scientific method"—the system of induc-tive reasoning upon which modern science is built. In contrast to earlier philoso-phers, like Aristotle and Plato, Bacon's methodology was based on experimentation, gathering of data, and prudent analysis, in order to uncover nature's essence. Loren Eisley, in a biography of Francis Bacon—*The Man Who Saw through Time* (1961), wrote that "more fully than any man of his time, [Bacon] entertained the idea of the universe as a problem to be solved, examined, meditated upon, rather than as an eternally fixed stage upon which man walked." In Bacon's own *Novum Organum* ("new method") that was published in 1620, he wrote that *the scientific method* would "eventually disclose and bring into sight all that is most hidden and secret in the universe."

Toward a Scientific Revolution

By the 19th century, the enormity of Renaissance ideas on nature and the physical world were realized to be part of a "scientific revolution." The philosophical framework for this revolution was Francis Bacon's methodology for scientific inquiry—*the scientific method*—establishing a research tradition for systematic experimentation. Many historians consider the publication of Nicolaus Copernicus' *De revolutionibus orbium coelestium* ("On the Revolutions of Heavenly Spheres") in 1543, to mark the beginning of the "scientific revolution," and the publication of Issac Newton's *Principia* in 1687—to mark its completion. During this period, a fundamental transformation of ideas occurred across the sciences (physics, astronomy, and biology) and an altered world view of the universe.

© ArTono/Shutterstock.com

For nearly 5000 years, astronomers had believed that the Earth lay at the center of the universe—a "geocentric model." Copernicus developed a "heliocentric model"—proposing that the Sun lies at the center of the universe, and that the Earth is just one of a number of planets that orbit the Sun. Discoveries and observations by the famed scientists—Johannes Kepler, Tycho Brahe, and Galileo Galilei—gave credence to Copernicus' idea. By the 17th century, the heliocentric model was accepted by most astronomers, and fully supported by the work of Isaac Newton. Newton's *Principia*, published in 1687, describes the laws of motion, and the law of universal gravitation—guiding principles that explain planetary motion, as well as the phenomena of tides and the trajectories of comets.

To those outside the scientific community, the rumblings of a "revolution" were also noted. In 1611, John Donne, the English poet, expressed a sentiment of revolutionary changes in world view in his verse:

> *The new Philosophy calls all in doubt,*
> *The Element of fire is quite put out;*
> *The Sun is lost, and th' earth, and no man's wit*
> *Can well direct him where to look for it.*

Leonardo Da Vinci

During the Renaissance, science and art were not disparate fields, but rather were considered to inform one another. The epitome of a "Renaissance Man"—Leonardo da Vinci (1452–1519)—skillfully bridged the overlap of art and science. He was an artist, anatomist, botanist, engineer, mathematician, physicist, and zoologist. Like other Renaissance artists, Leonardo realized that only a true understanding of human anatomy could lead to a life-like portrayal of figures. Under the tutelage of the prominent artist, Andrea del Verrochio (1435–1488), Leonardo performed dissections and garnered the artistic style of the Renaissance—rendering life as it is. Developing the powerful tools of observation and experimentation, Leonardo tried to uncover the mechanism that granted movement to organisms, and to establish a concept of life itself. Some contemporary scientists consider Leonardo to be a different type of "scientist" from Galileo or Newton—creating a more holistic and integrated body of knowledge, which might be considered a fore-runner to modern systems theory.* Leonardo viewed the human body as an analogy to the workings of the universe itself. In his rendition of *The Vetruvian Man* (Figure _____), which depicts a human figure inscribed inside both a square and a circle, Leonardo exhibits his interest in proportion as well as his ability to fuse scientific and artistic sensibilities.

Philosophically, Leonardo was a "Humanist" who believed in working to improve the lives of people rather than focusing on the otherworldly interests of the Church. Renaissance Humanists rebelled against Medieval Christianity, which idealized the ascetic lifestyle of the monk; they instead embraced the Renaissance man as one who lives in the moment for the betterment of humanity.

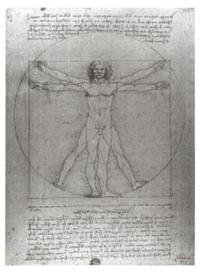

*Capra, Fritjof. *The Science of Leonardo: Inside the Mind of the Genius of the Renaissance.* New York: Doubleday (2007).

Pierre Belon

The concept of "homology"—the similarity between structures on different organisms that share common evolutionary origins—emerged during the Renaissance. The French biologist Pierre Belon (1517–1564) did extensive comparative studies—detailing skeletal similarities between disparate creatures like fish and mammals. Typical of Renaissance scholars, Belon's interests overlapped a number of disciplines, including zoology, botany, and classical antiquity, on which he wrote several scientific books. His work is cited as one of the earliest presentations of ideas on comparative anatomy. One of Belon's most in-depth analyses was a comparison of humans and birds in: *L'Historie de la nature des oyseaux* (1551)—where he pointed out their homologies in skeletal components and musculature. (Figure ___).

A few hundred years later, "homology" became an important element in Darwin's evolutionary theory, supporting the concept of "descent with modification." Exemplifying the homology of vertebrate forelimbs, in *The Origin of Species* (1859), Darwin wrote:

> "What can be more curious than that the hand of a man, formed for grasping, that of a mole for digging, the leg of the horse, the paddle of the porpoise, and the wing of the bat, should all be constructed on the same pattern, and should include the same bones, in the same relative positions?"

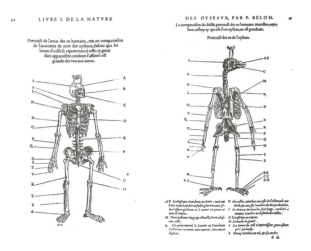

Andreas Vesalius

Another provocative Renaissance work on anatomy was Andreas Vesalius' *De humani corporis fabrica* ("On the Fabric of the Human Body"), published in 1543. Vesalius' text on human anatomy advanced the field of study at a time when human dissection was becoming a prominent component of medical education. Vesalius regarded his work as the first important revision on human anatomy since the work of Galen (the ancient Greek physician and philosopher whose ideas had dominated Western medicine for over 1300 years). While attending medical school at the University of Paris, Vesalius became increasingly critical of his professors who espoused Galen's teachings—stating that one could learn more anatomy from a butcher shop than from those who clung to the antiquated ideas of Galen.

While Vesalius' *Fabrica* bore some misguided information—the work was significant in describing the human body in a "modern" context, without relying on ancient texts. The first book of the *Fabrica* describes the human skeleton as a source of structural support for the entire body; the second book discusses musculature; the third book focuses on the vascular system; and the fourth book details the nervous system. Vesalius' ideas on anatomy were part of a period of rapid progress in European medicine (from 1400 to 1700) that is sometimes referred to as the "Medical Renaissance."

© Everett Historical/Shutterstock.com

William Harvey

The English physician/physicist William Harvey (1578–1657) was another prominent voice in the "Medical Renaissance"—contributing to a modern understanding of the human heart and circulatory system. Harvey is considered to be the first scientist in the Western world to provide quantitative evidence for the circulation of blood throughout the body. In 1616, Harvey first lectured on the human circulatory system at the Royal College of Physicians, in England, and then in 1628 published his *Exercitatio Anatomica de Motu Cordis et Sanguinis* ("Anatomical Treatise on the Movement of the Heart and Blood"). Although Harvey's text was only 72 pages long, it had a massive impact on the development of modern medicine and biology.

He was forthcoming in this work, describing the difficulties in his research—which involved performing vivisections on diverse animals, from eels to pigeons, in order to comprehend the vertebrate circulatory system.

> "When I first gave my mind to vivisections, as a means of discovering the motions and uses of the heart, and sought to discover these from actual inspection, and from the writings of others, I found the task to be truly arduous . . . that I was almost tempted to think . . . that the motion of the heart was only to be comprehended by God."

Despite these difficult moments, Harvey developed an accurate portrayal of the heart—disproving earlier notions that it did not contain muscle, and establishing that the heart is itself a muscle that circulates blood through regular, periodic contractions. Harvey decoded the direction of blood flow from the heart to the arteries of the body via contraction of the left ventricle, and realized the right ventricle's role in pumping blood to the lungs via the pulmonary artery.

In his later work, Harvey also contributed to the understanding of the embryo's developmental stages that he described in his book, *Exercitationer de Generatione Animalium* (1651). Here he replaced the earlier prevailing concept of "spontaneous generation" with the doctrine—*omne vivum ex ovo*—"all life comes from the egg." The concept of spontaneous generation was not entirely put to rest until the 19th century with the experimental evidence of Louis Pasteur.

CHAPTER 7
The 17th and 18th Centuries—Classification, Microscopes, and Fossils

In the 17th and 18th centuries, as Europe shifted from an agrarian to an industrialized society, the study of natural science was transformed. A new scientific philosophy—experimentally based, became the hallmark of European "scientific societies" or "academies." It differed from the ancient, more abstract work of Plato's Academy and Aristotle's Lyceum. While philosophers, like Rene Descartes (1596–1650) and Francis Bacon (1561–1639), provided a rationale for the new academies, scientists like Galileo and Harvey, guided the experimental approach and innovations like the microscope, telescope, and thermometer, made scientific investigations possible.

Of the many academies that cropped up in Europe and the United States during this period, the *Royal Academy of Sciences* in Paris and the *Royal Society of London* were among the most notable. In the United States, scientific societies were modeled after the *Royal Society of London* (the primary scientific advisor of the British government), but remained independent of government ties. In 1863, the *National Academy of Sciences* became the United States government's official institution for advisement on scientific issues.

Innovative instrumentation gave way to innovative ideas. And despite, Galileo's logic, "that anyone can see through my telescope," an elaborate 'dance' developed between scientists and their instruments—offering novel insights about the world—from the heavens to microscopic life.

Antonie van Leeuwenhoek

Referred to as the "Father of Microbiology," Antonie van Leeuwenhoek (1632–1723) revealed a world of microorganisms, previously unknown. Leeuwenhoek's revelation of microscopic life—what he referred to as "animalcules" (little animals), developed through his skill in lens-crafting, ultimately enabling him to create a microscope that could magnify objects 400 times. With the use of his microscopes, Leeuwenhoek became the first to record observations of protozoa, bacteria, and sperm cells, as well as the movement of blood through capillaries, and the fine structure of muscle tissue. Although Leeuwenhoek was not a formally educated scientist, he established communications with the Royal Society of London through a friend—Regnier de Graaf, a prominent Dutch physician. Once the Royal Society became aware of Leeuwenhoek's work, a close correspondence developed, and over the course of his life, Leeuwenhoek wrote hundreds of letters to the Society detailing his work in microscopy.

The microscopes that Leeuwenhoek crafted were relatively small hand-held devices, about 5 centimeters in length. The lens was placed close to the eye while looking into the light; on the other side of the lens, the sample was attached by a pin, and controlled by three screws that could alter the position and focus of the sample. Although several of Leeuwenhoek's microscopes have survived, he was private about sharing his lens-crafting techniques with the public, stating that there are aspects of microscope construction "that I keep only for myself."

Leeuwenhoek's visualizations of microscopic life forms, including sperm cells and larvae, led him to formulate pioneering ideas on animal and plant life cycles. He was convinced that even the smallest organisms were produced by parent organisms—casting doubt on the belief in spontaneous generation—that given an appropriate, environment organisms spontaneously emerge. (For example, frogs were thought to spontaneously emerge in swamplands, and maggots on rotting meat.) It was not until the 19th century, through the work of Louis Pasteur, that these ideas were conclusively disproven.

Carolus Linnaeus

© Georgios Kollidas/Shutterstock.com

The modern scientific system of classifying and naming organisms was developed by the 18th-century Swedish botanist and physician Carolus Linnaeus (1707–1778). Linnaeus' seminal work, *Systemae Naturae* (1735), provided an organized and concise means of naming species—known as *binomial nomenclature*. According to this system, every species is given a two-part name, the first term being the **genus** that the organism belongs to and the second term an **adjective** that is descriptive of the **species**. For example, the gooseberry plant, *Physalia angulata,* is in the genus *Physalia,* while the second name *angulata* describes its angular fruit. Prior to Linnaeus' binomial nomenclature, this plant was given the extensive scientific name of—*Physalia annua ramosissima ramis angulosis glabris foliis dentate-serratis.* Linnaeus also established a taxonomic hierarchy for the classification of organisms, where groups of similar species comprise genera (plural of genus), genera are grouped into orders, orders grouped into classes, and classes grouped into kingdoms. Later, biologists added two more intermediate taxonomic levels to the hierarchy—**family** falling between order and genus, and **phylum** falling between order and kingdom. More recently, the taxonomic level—the **domain,** has been added above kingdom—to designate the ancient divergence between bacterial type prokaryotic cells (without a nuclear membrane) and the more recently evolved eukaryotic organisms (whose cells have a nuclear membrane).

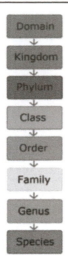

The Modern Taxonomic Hierarchy, based on Linnaeus' system.

Although Linnaeus viewed his task as naturalist—one of marveling at the work of the Creator and cataloguing God's creations—his system of taxonomic classification was adaptable to inclusion of evolutionary relationships among organisms as biology came to encompass these ideas. While Linnaeus considered humanity to be part of nature, and even described a continuum between apes and humans he believed that humanity had the divine right to dominate and improve the Earth. However, it was in his studies of plants, that Linnaeus thought he had found the "very footsteps of the Creator"—and he provided detailed and poetic descriptions of plant reproduction—that he referred to as a "celebration of love" in the plant world. Linnaeus systematically classified plants according to their reproductive organs and sex life—dividing plants into *classes* based on the number and type of stamens (male reproductive structures in flowers), and into *orders* based on the number and character of the pistils (female reproductive structures in flowers).

In a more practical vein, Linnaeus tried to apply his botanical knowledge to averting famine in Scandinavia in the 18th century—which was particularly problematic among the peasant classes. Linnaeus advised farmers whose crops had failed, to utilize native plants such as acorns, Iceland moss, seaweed, burdock, and thistles. He also hoped to "train" commercially important plants such as rice, tea, and olives to adapt and grow in the cold Scandinavian climate—leading to greater economic self-sufficiency for Sweden. Unfortunately, Linnaeus' economic schemes had limited success.

Comte de Buffon

Among the naturalists of the 18th century, Georges-Louis Leclerc, Comte de Buffon (1707–1788), epitomizes the revolutionary changes in the study and interpretation of nature that were part of an 18th-century Enlightenment. The Enlightenment undermined the authority of the monarchy and the church. It was built on the earlier 16th and 17th century Scientific Revolution—which was philosophically driven by scholars like Francis Bacon (1562–1626), Rene Descartes (1596–1650), John Lock (1632–1704), and Sir Isaac Newton (1642–1727). Buffon realized that in order to interpret the natural world, he needed to understand its history. Despite criticism from the church, he relied on the work of Newton, rather than the Bible, to conjecture how matter in motion may have given rise to the Earth. Buffon estimated that the Earth was about 70,000 years old—and while falling short of the contemporary figure of 4.5 billion years—it significantly lengthened and diverged from a biblical date of less than 7,000 years. To circumvent scriptural authority, Buffon interpreted the seven days of creation as seven epochs of undefined length—the first epoch encompassing the creation of the Earth, and the seventh epoch spanning the appearance of humanity.

Buffon proposed that life, like the Earth, has a history. Although he believed that organisms could spontaneously generate under the right conditions, he saw relationships between life forms inhabiting diverse geographic regions. In his day, elephant fossils had already been unearthed from Siberia and North America, and Buffon attributed their more recent geographic distribution in Africa and South Asia to migrations. He believed that the Siberian species gave rise to modern elephants, while the North American elephants had become extinct. It was during migrations, as species moved to new habitats, that Buffon envisioned their forms changing. He didn't think that migration could account for the development of radically new body plans—but rather could explain the geographic distribution of similar species. Buffon's ideas might be described as proto-evolutionary, which spurred new thoughts in the fields of comparative anatomy, geology, physics and natural history. In response to Buffon's writings, where he minimalized the presence of large animals in the Americas—Thomas Jefferson wrote *Notes from Virginia,* where he described, at length, the significant size of many North American mammals. Jefferson even shipped skeletons of several large moose, elk , and deer to Paris, to showcase the "immensity of many things in America." Both Thomas Jefferson and Benjamin Franklin visited Europe during this time, contributing to the scientific and political debates of the Enlightenment.

Erasmus Darwin

Erasmus Darwin (1731–1802), was an English physician, natural philosopher, and poet, and the grandfather of the revolutionizing biologist, Charles Darwin, credited with developing evolutionary theory. The elder Darwin was intrigued by the 18th-century idea that change in organic forms was possible, and that unlimited progress in society was also possible. He founded the Lichfield Botanical Society—established with the goal of translating the writings of Linnaeus, from Latin into English. This resulted in two primary publications—*A System of Vegetables* (1785) and *The Families of Plants* (1787). In these works Erasmus Darwin established many of the English plant names that are still in use today.

Zoonomia (1796) is considered to be Erasmus Darwin's most notable writing, where he foreshadowed some of the concepts of modern evolutionary theory developed by his grandson, Charles Darwin. In *Zoonomia,* Erasmus Darwin proposes a hypothesis on the transmutation of species—describing all life forms as descendants of a primordial "filament":

Would it be too bold to imagine that in the great length of time, since the Earth began to exist, perhaps millions of ages before the commencement of the history of mankind, would it be too bold to imagine that all warm-blooded animals have arisen from one living filament, which THE GREAT FIRST CAUSE endued with animality, with the power of acquiring new parts, attended with new propensities, directed by irritations, sensations, volitions, and associations, and thus possessing the faculty of continuing to improve by its own inherent activity and of delivering down those improvements by generation to its posterity, world without end!

Erasmus Darwin also alluded to a prototype of natural selection—later championed by Charles Darwin as the mechanism driving evolution—when he wrote in *Zoonomia* that every organism has "three great objects of desire—lust, hunger, and security." In another passage, paralleling the concept of "survival of the fittest," Erasmus Darwin wrote that "the strongest and most active animal should propagate the species, which should thence become improved." Although today Erasmus Darwin's writings gain most attention as a prelude to his grandson's work—at the time of their publication, the elder Darwin's books were considered "threatening" to religious ideas, and placed on an "Index of Prohibited Books" in England. Nonetheless, their impact was significant, and *Zoonomia* was translated into several languages and became very popular among German philosophers. Charles Darwin claimed to have read it twice, and the work had a significant influence on his own evolutionary thinking.

As a poet, Erasmus Darwin also expressed his botanical and biological thoughts in verse. In a stanza from the popular poem, "The Love of the Plants," published in 1789, he describes the sunflower—*Helianthus:*

GREAT HELIANTHUS guides o'er twilight plains
In gay solemnity his Dervise-trains;
Marshall'd in _fives_ each gaudy band proceeds,
Each gaudy band a plumed Lady leads;
With zealous step he climbs the upland lawn,
And bows in homage to the rising dawn;
Imbibes with eagle-eye the golden ray,
And watches, as it moves, the orb of day.

In explanatory notes, included with the verse, Erasmus Darwin explored his poetic references—describing the number and structure of the flower parts and the particular way in which the sunflower responds to the Sun by "nutation"—the circular swaying movement of the tip of a growing shoot.

- Explanatory Notes:

  [_Helianthus_. Sun flower. The numerous florets, which
  constitute the disk of this flower, contain in each five males
  surrounding one female, the five stamens have their anthers connected
  at top, whence the name of the class "confederate males;" see note on
  Chondrilla. The sun-flower follows the course of the sun by nutation,
  not by twisting its stem. Other plants, when they are
  confined in a room, turn the shining surface of their leaves, and bend
  their whole branches to the light. See Mimosa.]

© song_mi/Shutterstock.com

Georges Cuvier on Fossils

During the 18th century, fossils became scientifically recognized as the remains of living organisms that were not produced by the rocks they were imbedded in. As more fossils were unearthed, some appeared to resemble living species, while others looked distinct from contemporary life forms. Already noted in Buffon's day, elephants had left fossils in Europe and North America where they were no longer found, but elephants still lived in Africa and South America. Naturalists speculated that other fossils probably had living counterparts in distant regions as well. It was the French naturalist Georges Cuvier (1769–1832) who presented the radical idea

that some species had vanished from the Earth. In Cuvier's day, the idea of extinction was religiously troubling to much of society. According to religious views, God had created life according to a divine plan, and there was no rationale for why forms should die out. In the "Great Chain of Being," there was a continuum of life from ocean slime to humans; extinction would remove integral links.

In 1795, Georges Cuvier joined the National Museum in Paris as a leading expert on animal anatomy, and applied his knowledge to sorting out fossils. With great skill and accuracy, he reconstructed the anatomy of previously unknown species, sometimes utilizing only a few fragments of bone. Cuvier compared elephant fossils unearthed near Paris, with those from Siberia, and found clear differences between the two. He also determined that fossil elephant bones were distinct from those of living elephants in Africa and India. Cuvier scoffed at the rebuke by other naturalists—that in time, living members of fossil elephant species would be found in remote regions. He insisted that they were too big to miss! Based on his fossil studies, Cuvier proposed that the Earth periodically undergoes abrupt climatic changes, which wipe out species. His ideas on extinction strongly influenced Charles Darwin. However, Darwin, like the celebrated 18th-century geologist Charles Lyell who determined that the Earth undergoes significant physical changes, believed that extinctions occur gradually over time, rather than during sudden catastrophic events. This debate on gradual versus sudden extinctions has been revisited many times by contemporary biologists and paleontologists too. The current thought is that most species disappear gradually as "background extinctions," but that several times in the past 600 million years, "mass extinctions" occurred, where at least half of all living species disappeared within two million years (a short time in the geological time scale, which spans 3.5 billion years of life on the Earth). Catastrophes that precipitated mass extinctions included events such as asteroid impacts with the Earth, rapid changes in sea level, and volcanic eruptions. A great extinction marks a significant transition in life forms, where the disappearance of previous species leaves open niches for new species to fill. The rise of the mammals, and ultimately humanity, is directly linked to the mass extinction event that occurred 65 million years ago—wiping out extensive groups of organisms including the dinosaurs, which had been the dominant land vertebrates.

© Alta Oosthuizen/Shutterstock.com

Jean Baptiste de Lamarck

© Pidgorna Ievgeniia/Shutterstock.com

Jean Baptiste Pierre Antoine de Monet, Chevalier de Lamarck (1744–1829) was a forerunner of both cell theory and evolutionary theory—who recognized that life forms change in response to their environment. While Lamarck is often remembered for the hypothesis—Inheritance of Acquired Characteristics (that physical changes via use and disuse of body parts are heritable), which was later largely disproven—his influence on biological thought was significant. He was the first to develop a fully cohesive concept of evolution, realizing that organisms adapt to their environment. Charles Darwin credited Lamarck with being a great naturalist who inspired some of his own ideas on evolution, and in 1861 wrote of him:

> Lamarck was the first man whose conclusions on the subject [of evolution] excited much attention. This justly celebrated naturalist first published his views in 1801 . . . arousing attention to the probability of all changes in the organic, as well as inorganic world, being the result of law, and not of miraculous interposition.

Lamarck began his career as a naturalist with an interest in botany—publishing *Flore francoise* (1778)—a three-volume work on plants, which gained him membership into the French Academy of Sciences in 1779. He subsequently began studying animals, particularly invertebrates, and in 1793, when the Museum National d'Histoire Naturelle opened, Lamarck was given a professorship in zoology. In 1801, he published a definitive work on the classification of invertebrates, *Systeme des animaux sans vetebres*, where he introduced new categories of invertebrates—echinoderms, arachnids, crustaceans and annelids. Lamarck was also the first biologist to classify insects separately from arachnids (spiders, ticks, etc.), and to place crustaceans (crabs, lobsters, crayfish, etc.) in a distinct class from insects.

Lamarck's controversial concept on the mechanism that adapts organisms to the environment—the use or disuse of body structures—he stated in two laws.

> "First Law: In every animal which has not passed the limit of its development, a more frequent and continuous use of any organ gradually strengthens, develops and enlarges that organ, and gives it a power proportional to the length of time it has been so used; while the permanent disuse of any organ imperceptibly weakens and deteriorates it, and progressively diminishes its functional capacity, until it finally disappears."

> "Second Law: All the acquisitions or losses wrought by nature on individuals, through the influence of the environment in which their race has long been placed, and hence through the influence of the predominant use or permanent disuse of any organ; all these are preserved by reproduction to the new individuals which arise, provided that the acquired modifications are common to both sexes, or at least to the individuals which produce the young."

The concept expressed in Lamarck's second law is now referred to as "soft inheritance." This idea was considered to be largely disproven by modern genetics, and the work of August Weismann in the 1880s. Weismann cut the tails off mice for many generations and found that even after one-hundred or more generations the mice were born with tails as long as the first generation mice. However, recent developments in the field of *epigenetics* indicates that soft inheritance can play a role in changing an organism's phenotype—not by altering its DNA, but by preventing the expression of genes—this can be heritable to some degree. These new insights in molecular biology have led contemporary biologists to reconsider Lamarckian processes in evolution. Stephen Jay Gould a prominent 20th-century evolutionist has argued that Lamarck was the "primary evolutionary theorist" and set the tone for modern evolutionary theory.

Lamarck summed up his own ideas on evolution at a lecture given at the Musee National d'Histoire Naturelle, Paris, in 1803 where he stated:

> "Do we not therefore perceive that by the action of the laws of organization . . . nature has in favorable time, places, and climates multiplied her first germs of animality, given place to developments of their organizations . . . and increased and diversified their organs?
>
> Then . . . aided by much time and by a slow but constant diversity of circumstances, she has gradually brought about in this respect the state of things which we now observe. How grand is this consideration, and especially how remote is it from all that is generally thought on this subject."

Chapter 8
In the Light of Evolution—
Biology Comes of Age in the
19ᵗʰ Century

In 1859, with the publication of Charles Darwin's book, *The Origin of Species*, biology became a modern science. Lagging behind the physical sciences, which entered the modern age in the 17ᵗʰ century with the work of Galileo, the biological sciences finally gained a unifying theory through Darwin's text. *The Origin of Species* proposed that all life forms are related to one another by common descent and have changed over time through *Natural Selection*—a process that adapts organisms to their environment. Darwin detailed how nature, rather than a deity, selects the organisms best able to survive. The inherent greatness of Darwin's work was not just in his ideas, but in their presentation. He gave detailed accounts of natural phenomena, based on observations, and followed this with a synthesis of ideas. Darwin was a great synthesist—having the ability to see relationships between seemingly unrelated events. While other 19th-century developments in biology, such as bacteriology and physiology, may have had more immediate applications to human life, it was evolution that most significantly impacted on human thought. This final shift from a static view of life, to one of dynamic change—evolution, was one of the greatest intellectual revolutions of all time. Darwin ultimately gained an international reputation as one of the most influential figures in human history.

Other great ideas in 19th-century biology were the development of Cell Theory—that all life forms are composed of cells, and that cells arise only from pre-existing cells—and Mendelian genetics—that cast light on the inheritance of traits via discrete "particles"—that we now refer to as *genes*. Significant developments also took place in the realm of microbiology, with the work of scientists like Louis Pasteur.

Cell Theory (Schleiden and Schwann)

The commonplace idea that life is cellular was not "common" until the mid-19th century. The botanist Matthias Jacob Schleiden (1804–1881) and the animal physiologist Theodor Schwann (1810–1882) were prominent biologists of their generation, who in collaboration with one another, derived cell theory. Schleiden is often credited with the realization that all plants are cellular, and Schwann with the realization that all animals are cellular. These insights arose two-fold—first, Schleiden's description of the importance of the nucleus in the development of plant cells, and then Schwann's assessment, that the nucleus in animal cells performs the same function. The two scientists evaluated single-celled and multi-cellular plants and animals, establishing that the underlying cell structure is very similar in both the plant and animal kingdoms. It was in Schwann's *Microscopial Researches,* where the commonality in the cellular nature of all plant and animal tissue was first stated. Other 19th-century biologists, including Karl Nageli and Rudolph Virchow, forwarded the second tenet in modern cell theory that in the contemporary living world, *all cells arise from pre-existing cells.* (This does not address the origin of the earliest cells to appear on the Earth—which took place at a time when organic molecules could accumulate in the early seas in a pre-biotic soup—since there was little free oxygen in the atmosphere to break down organic molecules, and no pre-existing life forms to consume new organic material.) The work of Franz Leydid (1821–1902) and Robert Remak (1815–1865) clarified the role of the nucleus during cell division.

Louis Pasteur

Perhaps best remembered for developing the process of *pasteurization* (named for him), Louis Pasteur (1822–1895) was a renowned 19th-century French chemist and microbiologist. The pasteurization of beverages such as milk, wine, and beer became a commercially viable technique to destroy microbial contamination by heating liquids to a temperature between 60 and 100 degrees Celsius. Pasteur patented this technique in 1895 with the objective of "fighting the diseases of wine." He also made significant contributions to modern medicine, creating the first vaccines against rabies and anthrax, and developing a clinical application for the treatment of microbial-based diseases. Pasteur's work inspired a new generation of medical practitioners and surgeons, to develop antiseptic surgical techniques. In a speech at the Sorbonne in 1892, the eminent surgeon Joseph Lister described Pasteur's legacy:

> "Medicine owes not less than surgery to [Pasteur's] profound and philosophic studies. [He] raised the veil which for centuries has covered infectious diseases; [he] has discovered and demonstrated their microbic nature . . ."

In the realm of biology, Pasteur heralded a new understanding in the origin of life by disproving the belief in spontaneous generation—which held that given an appropriate environment, life forms will spontaneously appear. Pasteur's simple and elegant experiments, using sterile, sealed flasks, demonstrated that without microbial contamination, organisms do not *spontaneously* appear in a liquid broth. The experiments involved boiled broths contained in swan-necked flasks with a filter to prevent particles from entering the medium (Figure _____). Nothing grew in the flasks unless they were left open—indicating that organisms entered from outside the flask and did not "spontaneously" generate from within. Pasteur's stated conclusion from the experiment was that:

"Never will the doctrine of spontaneous generation recover from the mortal blow of this simple experiment. There is no known circumstance in which it can be confirmed that microscopic beings came into the world without germs, without parents similar to themselves."

Carried out under the auspices of the French Academy of Sciences, these experiments won Louis Pasteur, the Academy's prestigious Humbert Prize in 1862.

Charles Robert Darwin (1809–1882)

Charles Darwin's revolutionary ideas on evolution began with observations he made on a five-year journey around the globe—visiting locations around South America, Africa, and Australia, on a naval ship, the H.M.S. Beagle. In 1831, at the age of 23, having just graduated from Cambridge University with a degree in theology, Charles Darwin was invited to serve as "naturalist" on a British naval expedition set out to chart the coastal waters, primarily around South America. Darwin's official mission was to collect specimens for the British natural history museums, and to provide companionship for the captain, Robert FitzRoy. In the course of the five-year trip, Darwin visited many diverse environments, including the Brazilian rain forests, the Argentine pampas (grasslands), the Galapagos Islands (500 miles off the coast of Ecuador), numerous Pacific islands, Australia, New Zealand, Tahiti, and Southern Africa. While the Beagle staff was busy charting coastal waters, Darwin had the opportunity to go ashore for extended periods—collecting specimens, sometimes unearthing fossils, and recording observations.

At the time of Darwin's journey, "change was already in the air"—the budding science of geology was providing evidence that the Earth is substantially older than biblical accounts—and should be measured in billions of years rather than thousands

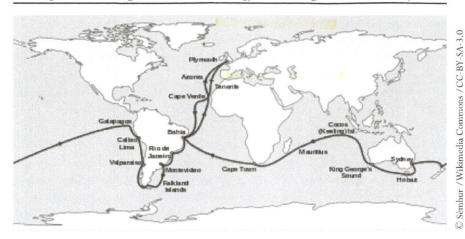

The Voyage of the Beagle, 1831–1836.

of years. Among Darwin's influential readings during the H.M.S. Beagle voyage was a three-volume work by the eminent geologist Charles Lyell—*Principles of Geology* (1830)—which provided scientific evidence for an ancient earth. This new geological timetable impacted on Darwin's view of the physical environment as he navigated novel landscapes. Lyell's insights led Darwin to understand that the Earth was very old and shaped by agents of change—weathering, erosion, glaciations, and volcanoes. While in South America, Darwin actually experienced an earthquake—giving him the realization that fossils of marine organisms can be lifted above sea level—and therefore, it is not unusual to find fossils of fish on mountain tops.

Darwin's ideas on biogeography (the geographic distribution of plants and animals) were shaped by his observations that South American organisms were different from those in Europe. Notably on the Galapagos Islands, Darwin found that bird species were distinct from one island to another. One of the most enduring analyses on speciation was the assessment of different species of Galapagos finches—that have since come to be known as "Darwin's finches." From a single species of South American mainland finch that had made its way to the Galapagos Islands, 13 species arose, each species with a variation in beak size and shape—an adaptation to utilizing seeds and insects, of varying size, for food. Darwin's observations of indigenous people in South America—who were culturally different from Europeans, led to him to realize that people also adapt to their environments. While Darwin saved most of his ideas on human evolution for a later book, *The Descent of Man* (1871)—it was during the Beagle expedition, that he began to formulate ideas on human adaptation as well.

Another formative read by Darwin was an essay, *On Population,* by the economist Thomas Malthus detailing how human populations grow, and grow—ultimately outgrowing their resources. Then, a famine ensues. Darwin related this concept to natural populations, realizing that in nature, populations grow beyond what their environment can support—setting up competition between organisms for food and other resources—"a struggle for survival." Those organisms that win out in the "struggle" are those with variations that give them an advantage in survival, while those with unfavorable variations are lost. It was this reasoning that led Darwin to propose the concept "survival of the fittest."

The field notes that Darwin recorded during his historic five-year expedition on the H.M.S. Beagle were developed into his first book—*Journal of Researches,* also known as *Voyage of the Beagle,* published in 1839. A second edition of this book, published in 1845, included some additional insights on evolution. The revised work was titled *Journal of Researches into the Geology and Natural History of the Various Countries Visited by H.M.S. Beagle Round the World.* In this new edition, Darwin highlighted his observations on the gradations in the size of the beaks in various species of finches on the Galapagos Islands. Alluding to the development of new species of *island* organisms from mainland species, he wrote:

© Anton_Ivanov / Shutterstock.com

> Considering the small size of these islands, we feel the more astonished at the number of their aboriginal beings, and their confined range . . . within a period geologically recent the unbroken ocean was here spread out. Hence, both in space and time, we seem to be brought somewhat near to that great fact—that mystery of mysteries—the first appearance of new beings on this earth.

Darwin reserved his completed theory on evolution for his book, *On the Origin of Species,* published on November 24, 1859. The title of this work in the first edition was *On the Origin of Species by Means of Natural Selection or the Preservation of Favoured Races in the Struggle for Life.* (In the sixth edition, the title was abbreviated to *The Origin of Species.*) Although Darwin had been working on this manuscript since his return from the Beagle journey in 1836, he had waited with its publication, perhaps due to a fear of invoking controversy with religious ideas on the origin of life. What ultimately spurred Darwin to publish *The Origin of Species* in November 1859 was a manuscript that he had received from a younger British naturalist Alfred Russell Wallace in 1858. Wallace had independently developed similar ideas to Darwin on evolution through natural selection, based on his own fieldwork in the Malay Archipelago in Indonesia. In the spring of 1858, Wallace's research was jointly presented with Darwin's at a meeting of the Linnean Society—the premier British scientific society. While historically Darwin has been credited with developing the *Theory of Evolution* via *Natural Selection*, Wallace was a significant voice—and some contemporary scientists choose to give joint credit by referencing—"Darwin's and Wallace's Theory of Evolution."

Gregor Mendel (1822–1884)

In the mid-19ᵗʰ century, at the same time that Charles Darwin was developing revolutionary ideas on evolution through natural selection, Gregor Mendel was developing revolutionary ideas on inheritance. However, Darwin and Mendel did not directly cross paths, and it was not until the early 1900s that Mendel's work was fully appreciated. While farmers, for centuries prior to Mendel, understood that crossbreeding plants or animals could result in desirable traits in offspring, it was through Mendel's controlled breeding experiments with pea plants that the laws governing inheritance were revealed.

Gregor Mendel, the "father of modern genetics," conducted crosses with the garden pea plant (*Pisum sativum*) while living as a monk at an Austrian monastery. Mendel was provided with a 4.9-acre experimental "backyard garden" on the monastery grounds. Initially, he began his breeding experiments with mice; however, the bishop at the monastery deemed it inappropriate for Mendel to be studying sex in animals—so he switched over to studying plants. In a humorous line from Mendel's biography, he is quoted as saying—"but little did *they* know, that plants have sex too."

© vvoe/Shutterstock.com

Mendel cataloged seven traits in pea plants that appeared to be inherited independently of other traits: plant height, seed shape, seed color, pod color, pod shape, flower color, and flower location on the plant. For each of these traits, he identified a dominant and recessive form—tall height was dominant over short height (which was recessive), and purple flower color was dominant over white flower color (which was recessive). Whenever a plant with the dominant form of the trait was crossed with a plant with the recessive form of the trait, the first generation offspring all had the dominant appearance (phenotype). However, when he crossed two first-generation "hybrid" plants, to produce a second generation cross, both the dominant and recessive phenotypes were seen in this next generation, in a ratio of 3 dominant to 1 recessive. These studies put into question the prevailing 19th-century view that inheritance takes place through a "blending" of traits (*Blending Inheritance*)—much the way colors of paint can be mixed together to form intermediate shades.

Despite compelling evidence for a "particulate theory" of inheritance—showing that discrete factors (*genes*) in combination with one another, dictate phenotype—Mendel's ideas were not accepted by the scientific community, until after 1900 when several other biologists began replicating and confirming his findings.

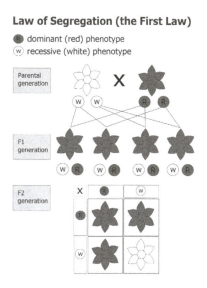

Law of Segregation (the First Law)

● dominant (red) phenotype
Ⓦ recessive (white) phenotype

CHAPTER 9
The Modern Synthesis and a World of DNA—Bringing It All Together in the 20th Century and Beyond

The Modern Synthesis

Modern evolutionary theory continued to develop since Darwin's time. The significance of *natural selection*, as the mechanism for evolutionary change, became fully realized in the 20th century. As evolution was fitted together with ideas on modern genetics in the 1930s and 1940s, a new evolutionary synthesis emerged—which came to be known as "The Modern Synthesis." It is this union of contemporary ideas on evolution, and the principles of inheritance, via Mendelian genetics, that forms the backbone of modern biology.

Thomas Hunt Morgan

The work of Thomas Hunt Morgan in his "Fly Room" at Columbia University beginning in the early 1900s highlighted the natural variation that exists in wild populations of organisms. Morgan collected wild fruit flies (*Drosophila melanogaster*), and identified many genetic variants that followed Mendelian inheritance patterns. Due to Morgan's success with *Drosophila*, laboratories throughout the world began studies on fruit flies—making *Drosophila* the first model organism for genetics. Although Morgan, early on, was a skeptic regarding natural selection as a driving force in evolution, his research ultimately supported Darwin's concept of evolution via natural selection, as well as Mendel's ideas on inheritance. Morgan concluded that:

> "The evidence shows clearly that the characters of wild animals and plants, as well as those of domesticated races, are inherited both in the wild and in domesticated forms according to Mendel's Law. Evolution has taken place

by the incorporation into the race of those mutations that are beneficial to the life and reproduction of the organism."

The research in Morgan's "Fly Room" contributed significantly to the new evolutionary synthesis that was emerging in the early 20ᵗʰ century.

DNA (Deoxyribonucleic acid)

The DNA story began many years before Watson and Crick elucidated the double-helix structure of the molecule in 1953—ultimately winning them a Nobel Prize in science. Their work was a culmination of the efforts of many notable scientists who established different aspects in understanding this complex molecule.

Friedrich Miescher, a Swiss physiological chemist, was the first to identify that nucleic acids existed—what he referred to as "nuclein" inside the nucleus of white blood cells. Originally believing that "nuclein" was a protein, which he extracted from human pus samples, Miescher was surprised to find that "nuclein" was resistant to processes of protein digestion, and that it had a much higher phosphorous content than any other "protein" he knew of. It was at this point that Miescher realized that he had come across a new substance. Foreshadowing the age of molecular genetics, he wrote:

> "It seems probable to me that a whole family of such slightly varying phosphorous-containing substances will appear, as a group of nucleins, equivalent to proteins."

Other 20ᵗʰ-century scientists followed Miescher's lead, and continued to investigate the chemical nature of "nuclein." One of these researchers was Phoebus Levene, a Russian biochemist, who is credited with several important insights about nucleic acids—that the three major components of a nucleotide are phosphate, sugar, and a base; that the sugar unit in RNA is ribose; and that the sugar unit in DNA is deoxyribose.

Erwin Chargaff, another prominent DNA researcher, built on Levene's revelations, and also the work of Oswald Avery, of Rockefeller University. In 1944, Avery and his colleagues had published a paper demonstrating that the "hereditary units— *genes*" are composed of DNA. Of this work, Chargaff wrote:

> "This discovery, almost abruptly, appeared to foreshadow a chemistry of heredity, and moreover, made probable the nucleic acid character of the gene . . . Avery gave us the first text of a new language, or rather he showed us where to look for it."

Chargaff's initial task was determining if there were differences in DNA among different species of organisms. In 1950, Chargaff reached the conclusion that the nucleotide composition of DNA differed from one species to another, but regardless of the species, he found one commonality—equivalencies between amounts of the four DNA nucleotides. The amount of *Adenine* always equaled *Thymine*, and the amount of *Cytosine* always equaled *Guanine*. This principle has come to be known as "Chargaff's Rule," and was one of the essential concepts that Watson and Crick utilized in garnering the structure of the DNA molecule.

Two British researchers, Rosiland Franklin and Maurice Wilkins, contributed to visualizing the three-dimensional structure of DNA through the development of a photographic technique known as X-ray crystallography. The helical configuration of the DNA molecule became evident through Franklin's and Wilkins's photographs, taken utilizing this technique.

James Watson, an American researcher, and Francis Crick, a British biochemist, collaborated—and putting all the pieces together, figuratively, and literally, built a three-dimensional model, which they revealed in 1953—elucidating the structure of DNA. Their Double-Helix Model was the final, definitive model of the structure of DNA. Watson and Crick's classic, paper describing the DNA double-helix was published in April, 1953, in the journal *Nature*.

> "We wish to put forward a **radically different structure for the salt of deoxyribose nucleic acid.** This structure has two helical chains each coiled round the same axis . . .
>
> The novel feature of the structure is the manner in which the two chains are held together by the purine [adenine; guanine] and pyrimidine [thymine; cytosine] bases. The planes of the bases are perpendicular to the fibre axis. They are joined together in pairs, a single base from one chain being hydrogen-bonded to a single base from the other chain, so that the two lie side by side . . . .
>
> It is found that only specific pairs of bases can bond together. **These pairs are: adenine (purine) with thymine (pyrimidine), and guanine (purine), with cytosine (pyrimidine).**
>
> In other words, if an adenine forms one member of a pair, on either chain, then on these assumptions the other member must be thymine; similarly for guanine and cytosine. The sequence of bases on a single chain does not appear to be restricted in any way. However, if only specific pairs of bases can be formed, it follows that if the sequence of bases on one chain is given, then the sequence on the other chain is automatically determined.
>
> **It has not escaped our notice** that the specific pairing we have postulated immediately suggests a possible copying mechanism for the genetic material."

The last line in this quotation from Watson and Crick's pivotal journal article— paved the way for an understanding of DNA replication and gene expression.

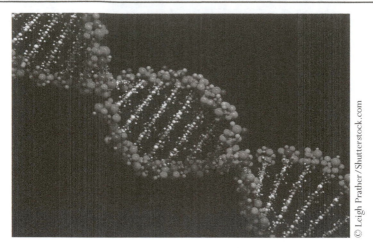

Watson and Crick with DNA model.

Watson and Crick, together with Maurice Wilkins (who had taken many of the photographic images of DNA), were awarded the Nobel Prize in Physiology and Medicine in 1962.

The Future

In the 21st century, we have entered the age of DNA technology—an outgrowth of understanding the structure and workings of DNA. There is an endless stream of applications—many practical, and in practice—like using bacterial cells as mini generators to produce pharmaceuticals. An example is how the human gene for insulin is inserted into bacterial chromosomes, and the genetically modified bacterial cells then produce human insulin, which is bottled as a medication. Genetically modified bacteria are used for environmental cleanup—breaking down crude oil after an oil spill. Transgenic plants resistant to pests have been developed and genes for growth hormone inserted into the egg cells of fish, cows, or sheep develop into larger animals. Since the first cloned mammal—Dolly the sheep, was born in 1997—numerous other organisms including goats, calves, and endangered animals have been cloned. And there are many more possibilities that nearly enter the realm of science fiction.

Natural history is a story without an end.

REFERENCES & SUGGESTED READINGS

Applebaum, W. ed. *Encyclopedia of the Scientific Revolution: From Copernicus to Newton.* New York: Garland Publications, 2000.

Aristotle. *Historia Animalium,* Richard McKeon, editor and translator. New York: Random House, 1941.

Avicenna. *A Treatise on the Canon of Medicine of Avicenna Incorporating a Translation of the First Book.* Trans. by O.C. Gruner. London: Luzac, 1930.

Bateson, W. *Mendel's Principles of Heredity—A Defense.* Cambridge, England: Cambridge University Press, 1902.

Carr, E. H. *What is History?* London: McMillan, 1961.

Chargaff, Erwin. "Chemical Specificity of nucleic acids and mechanism of their enzymatic degradation. *Experientia* 6: 201–209.

Darwin, Charles. *On the Origin of Species by Means of Natural Selection, or the Preservation of Favoured Races in the Struggle for Life.* London: J. Murray, 1859.

Darwin, Charles. *The Descent of Man.* London: Murray, 1871.

Darwin, Erasmus. "Loves of the Plants, a Poem with Philosophical Notes". Litchfield, 1789.

Darwin, Erasmus. *Zoonomia or the Laws of Organic Life.* 2 volumes. Dublin: P. Byrne and W. Jones, 1794.

Dobzhansky. T. "A critique of the species concept in biology." *Phil. Sci.* (1935) 2: 344–355.

Dobzhansky, T. *Genetics of the Evolutionary Process.* New York: Columbia University Press, 1970.

Futuyma, Douglas J. *Evolutionary Biology.* Sunderland, MA: Sinauer Associates, 1979.

Galen. *On the Usefulness of the Parts of the Body.* Trans. intro., and commentary by M. Tallmadge May. 2 vols. Ithaca, NY: Cornell University Press, 1968.

Gould, Stephen J. *Ontogeny and Phylogeny.* Cambridge: Harvard University Press, 1977.

Hippocrates' *Nature of Man, Humours, Aphorisms and Regimen.* Loeb Classical Library, vol. IV, W. H. S. Jones, translator. Cambridge: Harvard University Press, 1931.

Huxley, T.H. "The Physical Basis of Life," in *Evolution and Ethics and Other Essays,* D. Appleton, New York, 1909.

Leonardo da Vinci. *Leonardo da Vinci on the Human Body.* Translations, text, and introduction by C. D. O'Malley and J. B. de C. M. Sanders. New York: Dover, 1983.

Linnaeus, Carolus. *Systemma Naturae,* 10th edition. Stockholm: L. Salvii, 1758–1759.

Lister, Joseph, speech delivered at the Sorbonne in 1892 on Pasteur's seventieth birthday.

Magner, Lois N. *A History of the Life Sciences.* New York: Marcel Dekker, Inc., 2002.

Mayr, Ernst. *The Growth of Biological Thought—Diversity, Evolution and Inheritance.* Cambridge: Harvard University Press, 1982.

Mendel, Johann (Gregor). "Versuche uber Pflanzen-hybriden". *Verh. Natur. Vereins Brunn* 4(1865): 3–57.

Morgan, Thomas H. *Evolution and Adaptation.* New York: Macmillan, 1903.

Morgan, Thomas H. "Sex Limited Inheritance in *Drosophila,"Science,* 1910, vol. 32, pp. 120–122.

Pasteur, Louis. "Memoir on the Organized Corpuscles Which Exist in the Atmosphere," Paris, 1896.

Plato. *Tinnaeus.* Translated with introduction by Donald J. Zeyl. Indianapolis, IN: Hackett Pub. Co., 2000.

Ritterbush, Philip C. *Overtures in Biology: The Speculation of Eighteenth Century Naturalists.* New Haven and London: Yale University Press, 1964.

Schleiden, Matthias. "On Phytogenesis," in Johannes Muller, *Archives for Anatomy and Physiology.*

Schwann, Theodor. "Microscopical Researches on the Similarity in Structure and Growth of Animals and Plants", London, The Sydenham Society, 1847.

Serafini, Anthony. *The Epic History of Biology.* Cambridge, MA: Perseus Publishing, 1993.

Seward, A. C. (ed.) *Darwin and Modern Science.* Cambridge: Cambridge University Press, 1909.

Singer, Charles. *A Short History of Scientific Ideas to 1900.* New York: Oxford University Press, 1959.

Vesalius, A. *The Epitome of Andreas Vesalius.* Translated by L.R. Lind and C.W. Asling. Cambridge, MA: MIT Press, 1969.

Watson, James D. and Francis Crick. "A Structure for Deoxyribose Nucleic Acid". *Nature,* 1953, vol. 171: 737–738.

Watson, James D. *The Double Helix.* New York: Atheneum, 1968.

Williams, G. C. *Adaptation and Natural Selection.* Princeton: Princeton University Press, 1966.

Wilson, C. *The Invisible World: Early Modern Philosophy and the Invention of the Microscope.* Princeton, NJ: Princeton University Press, 1995.

Wittgenstein, Ludwig. *Philosophical Investigations.* New York: McMillan, 1953.

Zagorin, P. *Francis Bacon.* Princeton, NJ: Princeton University Press, 1999.